STRUM & SING

DEAR EVAN HANSEN

Cover photo courtesy of Serino Coyne

ISBN: 978-1-5400-5533-0

HAL•LEONARD®

Visit Hal Leonard Online at
www.halleonard.com

Contact us:
Hal Leonard
7777 West Bluemound Road
Milwaukee, WI 53213
Email: info@halleonard.com

In Europe, contact:
Hal Leonard Europe Limited
42 Wigmore Street
Marylebone, London, W1U 2RN
Email: info@halleonardeurope.com

In Australia, contact:
Hal Leonard Australia Pty. Ltd.
4 Lentara Court
Cheltenham, Victoria, 3192 Australia
Email: info@halleonard.com.au

Anybody Have a Map?

Music and Lyrics by
Benj Pasek and Justin Paul

*Tune down 1/2 step:
(low to high) E♭ - A♭ - D♭ - G♭ - B♭ - E♭

Csus2   D5   G5   Gsus2   G/B   Em7   Dsus4

A7   Gmaj7(no3rd)   D   Am7   Am11   G

Intro

‖: Csus2   D5 | G5   Gsus2   :‖
| Csus2   D5 | G5   Gsus2 |
| G5   Gsus2

Verse 1

          ‖ Csus2   D5 | G5   Csus2 G/B
Can we try to have an optimistic out - look?
      | Csus2   D5
Can we buck up just e - nough to see…
      | G5   Csus2
The world won't fall apart?
      | Em7   Gsus2
Maybe this year we decide
      | Dsus4   Em7 |
We're not giving up be - fore we've tried.
Csus2 | G5   Gsus2 | G5   Gsus2   ‖
This year we make a new   start.

Interlude 1

| Csus2   D5 | G5   Gsus2 |
| Csus2   D5 | G5   Gsus2

*Optional to match recording

Verse 2

```
                    ‖Csus2        D5                    |G5      Csus2   G/B
Another stellar con - versation for the scrap - book.
                     |Csus2         D5
Another stumble as I'm reaching
                      |G5            Csus2
For the right thing to say.
                      |Em7            Dsus4
Well, I'm kinda comin' up empty,
                     |G/B    A7    |    G/B ‖
Can't find my way to you.
```

Chorus 1

```
Csus2              Dsus4
   Does anybody have a map?
                         |Gmaj7(no3rd)
Anybody maybe happen to know
Em7              D5       |Csus2
How the hell to do this?
                 Dsus4                    |G5
I dunno if you can tell, but this is me
        Gsus2    G/B    |Csus2
Just pretending to know.
                   D                    |G/B
So where's the map? I need a clue
        Csus2               |Am7
'Cause the scary truth is I'm flyin' blind
               |Csus2           N.C.   |G5      |          ‖
And I'm making this up as I go.
```

Interlude 2

```
                    (Capo 1st fret)
                    ‖:G5    Am11   Csus2    |                    :‖ Play 3 times
                    |G5
```

Verse 3

    ‖**Csus2**   **D5** |**G5**   **Csus2** **G/B**
Another masterful attempt ends with disas - ter.

    |**Csus2**   **D5**
Pour an - other cup of coffee

     |**Gsus2**   **Csus2**
And watch it all crash and burn.

  |**Em7**   **Gsus2**
It's a puzzle, it's a maze:

  |**Dsus4**   **Em7**
I try to steer through it a million ways

 |**Am7**   **Csus2** |**G5** **Gsus2** |**G5**   **G/B**‖
But each day's another wrong turn.

Chorus 2

Csus2   **Dsus4**
  Does anybody have a map?

     |**Gmaj7(no3rd)**
Anybody maybe happen to know

Em7   **D5** |**Csus2**
How the hell to do this?

    Dsus4 |**G5**
I dunno if you can tell, but this is me

  Gsus2 **G/B** |**Csus2**
Just pretending to know.

       D |**G/B**
So where's the map? I need a clue

   Csus2 |**Am7** |
'Cause the scary truth is I'm flyin' blind.

G/B |
I'm flyin' blind.

Csus2 |**D**
I'm flyin' blind and I'm making this up

  |**G** **A7** **Csus2** |
As I go, _____

  |**G** **A7** **Csus2** | |
As I go. _____

G   ‖

Waving Through a Window

Music and Lyrics by
Benj Pasek and Justin Paul

(Capo 2nd fret)

Intro
‖: G/B   Csus2   Dsus4 | :‖

Verse 1

G/B   Csus2   Dsus4| |G/B
     I've learned to slam on the brake

     Csus2 Dsus4| |G/B
Before I even   turn   the key,

     Csus2   Dsus4| |G/B
Before I make the mis - take,

     Csus2   Em | D   ‖
Before I lead with the worst of me.

Verse 2

G/B   Csus2   Dsus4| |G/B
     Give them no reason to stare.

     Csus2 Dsus4| |G/B
No slipping up   if you   slip away.

     Csus2   Dsus4| |G/B
So I got nothin' to share.

     Csus2   Em | D
No, I got nothin' to say.

Pre-Chorus 1

```
        A7sus4 ‖              |Em        D
                Step out, step outta the sun
            G/B |       Csus2      |        A7sus4 |
        If you keep gettin' burned.
                        |Em        D
        Step out, step outta the sun
            G/B |       Csus2
        Be - cause you've learned,
            D        |              |
        Be - cause you've learned.
```

Chorus 1

```
        Em7 ‖            Csus2 |
                On the outside,      always lookin' in.
            |G5              |Dsus4
        Will I      ever be more than I've always been?
                    |Em7             Csus2 |          |
        'Cause I'm tap-tap-tappin' on the        glass,
        G5            Dsus4 |
        Waving through a win - dow.
            Em7 |              Csus2 |
        I        try to speak but      nobody can hear
             |G5                  Dsus4 |
        So I      wait around for an an - swer to appear
                    |Em7                     Csus2 |          |
        While I'm watch-watch-watchin' peo - ple        pass.
             |G5              Dsus4 |     B7  Em7 |
        I'm waving through a win - dow, oh.
        Csus2 |      G5 |
        Can    anybody see?
                    |D            ‖
        Is anybody waving…
```

Interlude

```
Csus2   G5   Dsus4 |              | Csus2   G5   Dsus4 |                        ||
Back at me?
```

Verse 3

```
G/B              Csus2      Dsus4 |            | G/B
   We start with stars in our eyes.
                 Csus2      Dsus4 |            | G/B
We start be - lievin' that we       belong.
               Csus2      Dsus4 |            | G/B
But ev'ry sun doesn't rise
               Csus2          Em |    D        ||
And no one tells you where you went wrong.
```

Pre-Chorus 2

Repeat Pre-Chorus 1

Chorus 2

```
Em7 ||              Csus2  |
     On the outside,       always lookin' in.
       | G5           | Dsus4
Will I     ever be more than I've always been?
       | Em7             Csus2  |              |
'Cause I'm tap-tap-tappin' on the       glass,
G5            Dsus4 |
Waving through a win  -  dow.
 Em7 |               Csus2  |
I       try to speak but       nobody can hear
       | G5                 Dsus4 |
So I     wait around for an an  -  swer to appear
         | Em7                      Csus2  |         |
While I'm watch-watch-watchin' peo - ple        pass.
G5            Dsus4 |    B7   Em7 |
Waving through a win  -  dow, oh.
Csus2 |      G5  |
Can   anybody see?
             | D
Is anybody waving?
```

7

Bridge

```
N.C.              ‖ G/B            Csus2
When you're fallin' in a for - est
Dsus4       |         Em7
And there's nobody a - round,
         | G/B          Csus2
Do you ever really crash
   Dsus4 |          Em7
Or e  -  ven make a sound?
             | G/B            Csus2
When you're fallin' in a for - est
Dsus4       |         Em7
And there's nobody a - round,
         | G/B        Csus2
Do you ever really crash
   Dsus4 |          Em7
Or e  -  ven make a sound?
             | G/B            Csus2
When you're fallin' in a for - est
Dsus4       |         Em7
And there's nobody a - round,
         | G/B        Csus2
Do you ever really crash
   Dsus4 |          Em7
Or e  -  ven make a sound?
             | G/B            Csus2
When you're fallin' in a for - est
Dsus4       |         Em7
And there's nobody a - round,
         | G/B        Csus2
Do you ever really crash
   Dsus4 |          Em7
Or e  -  ven make a sound?
      | G/B        Csus2
Did I even make a sound?
   Dsus4 |          Em7
Did I       even make a sound?
      | G/B        Csus2
It's like I never made a sound.
      Dsus4 | N.C.
Will I       ever make a sound?
```

(Capo 3rd fret)

8

Chorus 3

Em7 ‖   Csus2 |
     On the outside,   always lookin' in
 |G5   Dsus4 |
Will I   ever be more   than I've always been?
     |Em7   Csus2 | |
'Cause I'm tap-tap-tappin' on the   glass,
G5   Dsus4 |
Waving through a win - dow.
 Em7 | Csus2 |
I   try to speak but   nobody can hear
 |G5   Dsus4 |
So I   wait around for an an - swer to appear
     |Em7   Csus2 | |
While I'm watch-watch-watchin' peo - ple   pass.
G5   Dsus4 | B7 Em7 |
Waving through a win - dow, oh.
Csus2 | G5 |
Can   anybody see?
     |Dsus4   ‖
Is anybody waving…

Outro

G/B   Csus2 Dsus4| |G/B
Back at me?
 Csus2   Dsus4 | |
Is   anybod - y   waving?
Em7   G5/F♯|
Waving.
     Csus2 |
Waving.
     |
Whoa,
 N.C. | G5 |Gsus2 | ‖
Whoa. _____

For Forever

Music and Lyrics by
Benj Pasek and Justin Paul

(Capo 5th fret)

C Cmaj7 Fmaj7 F6 Fmaj7sus2 Am G C/E Fsus2 C/G

D7 Gsus4 Bb Abadd9 Eb Cm F/A Dm F/C Gsus$\frac{2}{4}$

D Dmaj7 D/F# Gsus2 Bm7 D5/A Cadd9 E7 Em11 A7sus4

Verse 1

C   **|Cmaj7**
End of May, or early June, this   picture

     |Fmaj7   **|F6**   **|**
Perfect afternoon we share.

C   **|Cmaj7**
Drive the winding country road,

Grab a scoop at "A La Mode"

   |Fmaj7   **|F6**   **|**
And then we're there.

Fmaj7sus2
An open field that's framed with trees,

 | **|C**   **|**
We pick a spot and shoot the breeze like buddies do.

Fmaj7sus2   **|**
Quoting songs by our fav'rite bands,

                |C
Telling jokes no one understands ex - cept us two.

   |Am   **Fmaj7**   **|G**   **||**
And we   talk and take in the view.

Chorus 1

```
            C        Cmaj7    | C/E
               All we see is sky
     Fsus2
   For forever.
    | C        Cmaj7         | C/E
   We let the world pass by
     Fsus2            | Am
   For forever.
              C/G              | Fsus2
   Feels like we could go on
     C                    | D7
   For forever this way;
                  | Fsus2      Gsus4       ||
   Two friends          on a perfect day.
```

Interlude 1 | C | Cmaj7 | Fmaj7 | F6

Verse 2

```
            || C
   We walk a while and talk about
      | Cmaj7                           | Fmaj7         | C
   The things we'll do when we get out of        school.
                                | Cmaj7
   Bike the Appalachian Trail, or        write a book, or learn to sail.
            | Fmaj7
   Wouldn't that be cool?
            | Fmaj7sus2
   There's nothing that we can't discuss,
       |                              | C
   Like, girls we wish would notice us but never do.
      | Fmaj7sus2
   He looks around and says to me,
             |
   "There's nowhere else I'd rather be."
        | C
   And I say, "Me too."
            | Am    Fmaj7              | G
   And we talk   and     take in the view.
            | Am   Fmaj7  | G          ||
   We just talk and     take in the view.
```

C   Cmaj7 |C/E
All we see is sky

 Fsus2
For forever.

   |C   Cmaj7 |C/E
We   let the world pass by

 Fsus2 |Am
For forever.

     C/G |Fsus2
Feels like we could go on

  C |Fmaj7 B♭
For forever this way,

 |Fsus2 |C
This way.

    Cmaj7 |C/E
All we see is light

 Fsus2 |C
For forever.

     Cmaj7 |C/E
'Cause the sun shines bright

 Fsus2 |Am
For forever.

    C/G |Fsus2
Like we'll be alright

 C |D7
For forever this way:

     |Fsus2   Gsus4 |C
Two friends   on a perfect day.

Bridge

‖ A♭add9 E♭
And there   he goes
　　　|Cm　　　　B♭
Racin' toward the tall - est tree.
　　　|A♭add9 E♭
From far across a yellow field
　　|Cm　　　B♭　　　　　　|
I hear him call - in', "Follow me!"
　　　F/A　　　　　|
There we go wonderin'
Dm　　　　　C　　　　　　　　　|B♭
How the world might look from up so high.
　　　　　　　　　　　　|
One foot after the other.
　　　　　　　　　|C/E
One branch, then to another.
　　　　　　　　|
I climb higher and higher.
　　　　　　　　|Dm　　　|B♭　　　|
I climb 'til the entire sun shines on my face.
　|Dm　　C　　F/A　　|B♭
And I suddenly feel the branch give way.
　　　|F/A
I'm on the ground.
　　　|Am　　　Dm
My arm goes numb.
　　　|F/C
I look around
　　　|Gsus²₄
And I see him come to get me.
　|　　　　　　|B♭
He's come to get me,
　　　　　　　|C　　　　‖
And ev'rything's okay.

Chorus 3

```
 D      Dmaj7           |D/F♯
   All we see is the sky

 Gsus2
For forever.
      |D      Dmaj7        |D/F♯
We   let the world pass by.
 Gsus2        |Bm7
For forever.
      D5/A         |Gsus2
Buddy, you and I
      D              |Cadd9
For forever this way,
   |Gsus2      |D
This way.
      Dmaj7      |D/F♯  Gsus2    |D
All we see is light _____
         Dmaj7   |D/F♯ Gsus2   |Bm7
'Cause the sun burns bright.
      D5/A    |Gsus2
We could be alright
 D/F♯              |E7          |
For forever this way:
             |Em11
Two friends,
      |G      A7sus4          |D
True friends on a        perfect day.
|Dmaj7      |Gsus2      |A7sus4   |D            ‖
```

Sincerely, Me

Music and Lyrics by
Benj Pasek and Justin Paul

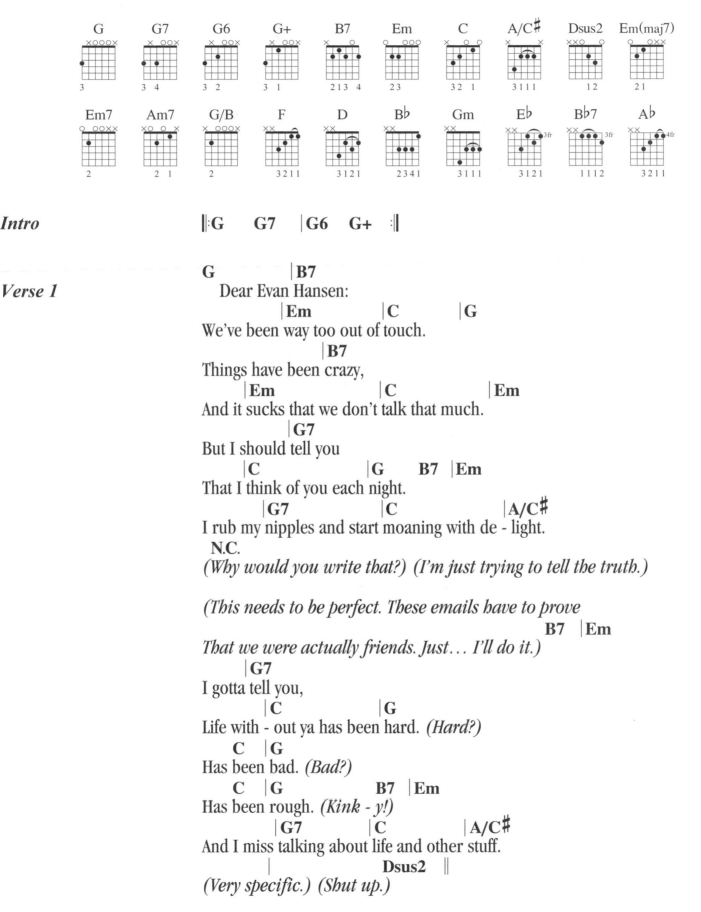

Intro   ‖: G   G7 |G6   G+ :‖

Verse 1

    G |B7
    Dear Evan Hansen:
        |Em |C |G
We've been way too out of touch.
         |B7
Things have been crazy,
    |Em |C |Em
And it sucks that we don't talk that much.
       |G7
But I should tell you
    |C |G   B7 |Em
That I think of you each night.
    |G7 |C |A/C♯
I rub my nipples and start moaning with de - light.
   N.C.
(Why would you write that?) (I'm just trying to tell the truth.)

(This needs to be perfect. These emails have to prove
                 B7 |Em
That we were actually friends. Just… I'll do it.)
    |G7
I gotta tell you,
     |C |G
Life with - out ya has been hard. *(Hard?)*
     C |G
Has been bad. *(Bad?)*
     C |G   B7 |Em
Has been rough. *(Kink - y!)*
     |G7 |C |A/C♯
And I miss talking about life and other stuff.
    | Dsus2 ‖
(Very specific.) (Shut up.)

Verse 2

```
G        |B7     N.C.        |G
    I like my parents, (Who says that?)
          |B7          |Em        |C        |G
I love my parents, but each day's another fight.
          |B7
If I stop smoking drugs,
     |Em          |C        B7 |
Then ev'rything might be alright.
                 |           Dsus2 |G
(Smoking drugs?) (Just fix it!)
          |B7      N.C.      |G
If I stop smoking crack, (Crack?)
          |B7
If I stop smoking pot,
     |Em          |C        B7 |Em
Then ev'rything might be alright.
        |Em(maj7)  |Em7
I'll take your advice,
          |A/C#       |Am7
I'll try to be more nice.
     G/B   |C       A/C#  |Dsus2      |          F ||
I'll turn it a - round, wait and see.
```

Chorus 1

```
           |C        |G   |        F |
'Cause all it takes is a little re - in - ven - tion.
           |C              |G   |        B7 |
It's easy to change if you give it your at - ten - tion.
           |Em        |D
All you gotta do is just be - lieve
           |G          |C
You can be who you wanna be.
     |G    D    ||
Sin - cere - ly,
```

Interlude

```
G      G7    |G6           G+          |G
Me. (Are we done yet?) (I can't just give them one email.
  G7         |G6      G+
I wanna show that I was, like,
        |G        G7        |G6   G+ ||
A good friend, you know?) (Oh, my God.)
```

16

Verse 3

```
G                      |B7
    Dear Connor Murphy:
   |Em           |C        |G
Yes, I also miss our talks.
           |B7              |Em
Stop doing drugs, just try to take deep breaths
   |C        B7        |Em
And  go on walks. (No.)
              |G7
I'm sending pictures
          |C           |G     B7  |Em
Of the most amazing trees. (No.)
                |G7
You'll be ob - sessed
            |C           |A/C♯               B7      |Em
With all my forest exper - tise. (Absolute - ly not.)
                  |Em(maj7) |Em7
Dude, I'm proud of you,
             |A/C♯            |Am7
Just keep push  - ing through.
        G/B          |C   A/C♯  |Dsus2
You're turning around, I can see.
                 |              F  ‖
Just wait and see.
```

Chorus 2

```
           |C          |G      |       F  |
'Cause all it takes is a little re - in - ven - tion.
            |C          |G       |      B7  |
It's easy to change if you give it your at - ten - tion.
              |Em           |D
All you gotta do is just be - lieve
              |G            |C
You can be who you wanna be.
      |G      D   |
Sin - cere - ly,
G   N.C.       |                            ‖
Me. My sister's hot. (What the hell?) (My bad.)
```

Verse 4

B♭ |D
Dear Evan Hansen:
       |Gm |E♭ |B♭
Thanks for ev'ry note you send.
       |D
Dear Connor Murphy:
       |Gm |B♭7 C |
I'm just glad to be your friend.
       |F |D
Our friendship goes beyond
       |Gm |C
Your av'rage kind of bond.
       |F |D
But not be - cause we're gay,
       |Gm   F |
No, not be - cause we're gay.
       |B♭
We're close but not that way.
  |A♭ |E♭ |F |N.C.
The only man that I love is my dad.
       |F | |
Well, any - way, you're getting better ev'ry day.
      | |G
I'm getting better ev'ry day.
       | | |
Keep getting better ev'ry day.
              F ‖
(Hey! Hey! Hey! Hey!)

Chorus 3

```
                 |C          |G    |          F |
'Cause all it takes is a little re - in - ven - tion.
                 |C               |G     |       B7 |
It's easy to change if you give it your at - ten - tion.
                |Em          |D
All you gotta do is just be - lieve
                |G          |C
You can be who you wanna be.
    |G    D    |
Sin - cere - ly…
C        |G    D |C
Miss you dear - ly.
    |G    D    ‖
Sin - cere - ly,
```

Outro

```
G    G7  |G6
Me.
    G+   |G    G7  |G6
Sin - cerely, Me.
    G+   |G    G7  |G6   G+  |G
Sin - cerely, Me. _____
N.C.     |     G   N.C. ‖
Sincerely, Me.
```

Requiem

Music and Lyrics by
Benj Pasek and Justin Paul

(Capo 2nd fret)

| Bm7 | D5 | G5 | Asus4 | Aadd4/C♯ | D/F♯ | Em7 | E7/G♯ | Cadd9 | G/B |

Intro ‖: **Bm7** | **D5 G5** | **Asus4** :‖

Verse 1

Bm7　　　**Aadd4/C♯**
Why should I play

D5 | **D/F♯**　　 | **G5**
This game of pre - tend,

　　| **Bm7**　　　**Aadd4/C♯**
Re - membering through

D5 | **D/F♯**　　　**G5** |　　　|
A　　secondhand sor - row?

Bm7　　　**Aadd4/C♯**
Such a great son

D5 | **D/F♯**　　**G5**　　　|
And wonder - ful friend,

　　| **Asus4** | **D/F♯**　**G5**　　　|　　　　‖
Oh, don't the tears　just pour?

Verse 2

Bm7   **Aadd4/C♯**
I could curl up
D5 |**D/F♯**   **G5** | |
And hide in my room,
Bm7   **Aadd4/C♯**
There in my bed
D5 |**D/F♯**   **G5** | |
Still sobbing to - mor - row.
Bm7   **Aadd4/C♯**
I could give in
D5 |**D/F♯** **G5** |
To all of the gloom
     |**Asus4** |
But tell me,
G5   **Asus4** | ||
Tell me what   for?

Pre-Chorus 1

Em7 | **Bm7** |
Why should I have a heavy heart?
G5 | **Asus4** |
Why should I start to break in pieces?
Em7 | **Bm7** |**Asus4** | ||
Why should I go and fall a - part for you?

Chorus 1

D5 | |
Why _____

            | |
Should I play the griev - ing girl and
Asus4 | |
   Lie, _____
          |
Saying that I miss you
      |**Bm7** | |**G5**
And that my world has gone dark
     | |**Asus4** | |
Without your light?
Em7 **D/F♯** |**E7/G♯** **G5** |
I will sing no requi - em…
         ||
Tonight.

Interlude

|**Bm7** |**D5** **G5** | **Asus4** |
|**Bm7** |**D5** **G5** | **Asus4**

Verse 3

```
   ‖Bm7              Aadd4/C♯
I  gave you the world,
   D5 |D/F♯      G5    |          |
You threw it away,
   Bm7           Aadd4/C♯  D5 |
Leaving these bro    -     ken
   D/F♯      G5  |          |
Pieces be - hind you.
   Bm7        Aadd4/C♯  D5 |
Ev'rything wast    -    ed,
   D/F♯      G5      |
Nothing to say,
    |Em7           |D/F♯
So I can sing no requiem.
```

Verse 4

```
     ‖Bm7       Aadd4/C♯
I  hear your voice
   D5 |D/F♯    G5   |
And feel you ___ near.
       |Bm7           Aadd4/C♯   D5 |
With - in these words I
   D/F♯  G5  |
Finally find you.
       |Bm7       Aadd4/C♯
And now that I know
   D5   |D/F♯  E7/G♯ |          |
That you are   still here,
   G5          |Asus4          ‖
I will sing no requiem tonight.
```

Pre-Chorus 2

```
   Em7               |    Bm7   |
Why should I have a heavy heart?
   G5                |        Asus4  |
Why should I say I'll keep you with me?
   Em7              |    Bm7  |Asus4   |          ‖
Why should I go and fall a - part for you?
```

Chorus 2   *Repeat Chorus 1*

Bridge

Asus4 | D/F# |G5
'Cause when the villains fall,
       | |Asus4 |
The king - doms never weep.
     D/F# |G5 | Em7 |Asus4
No one lights a candle to remem - ber.
    | D/F# |G5
No, no one mourns at all
       | |Asus4 |
When they lay them down to sleep.
    |Cadd9 |G5 |D5 |
So don't tell me that I didn't have it   right.
    |Cadd9 |G5 |D5 |
Don't tell me that it wasn't black and white.
    |Cadd9 |G/B
After all you put me through,
    |Cadd9 |G/B
Don't say it wasn't true,
    |Em7 | |G5 |
That you were not the mon - ster that I knew.

Chorus 3

    ||D5 | |
'Cause I _____

           | |Asus4
Cannot play the griev - ing girl and
          | |
Lie,
          | |Bm7 |
Saying that I miss you and that my world
    |G5 | |Asus4 | |
Has gone dark.
Em7 D/F# |E7/G# G5 | |
I will sing no requi - em,
Em7 D/F# |E7/G# G5 | |
I will sing no requi - em,
Em7 D/F# |E7/G# G5 |
I will sing no requi - em…

Outro

    ||Bm7 |
To - night.
D5   G5 | Asus4 |Bm7 |
Oh, _____   oh. _____
D5   G5 | Asus4 |Bm7 | ||
Oh, _____   oh. _____

If I Could Tell Her

Music and Lyrics by
Benj Pasek and Justin Paul

E5   A5   C#m7   F#7add4   Bsus4   Bsus4/A   Eadd9/G#   Asus2

F#m11   E   C(b5)   C   G   D   Em   Cadd9

G/B   B7   Am7   Dadd2/4   G5   A7sus4   Csus2

Intro

|E5 | |A5 | |
|E5 | |A5 | ||

Verse 1

E5 | |A5 |
He said there's nothing like your smile,

    |E5 | |A5 | |
Sort of subtle and perfect and real.

E5 | |A5 |
He said you never knew how wonderful

    |E5 | |A5 |
That smile could make someone feel.

Verse 2

    ‖E5 | |A5 |
And he knew when - ever you get bored,

        |E5 | |A5 |
You scribble stars on the cuffs of your jeans.

    |E5 | |A5 |
And he no - ticed that you still fill out the quizzes

        |E5 | |A5 |
That they put in those teen magazines.

Pre-Chorus 1

‖C#m7　　|F#7add4
But he kept　　it all

　　|Bsus4　Bsus4/A |Eadd9/G#
In - side　　　his　head.

　　　　　　|C#m7　　|F#7add4　　|Bsus4
What he saw,　　he left　　　　un - said.

　　　　　　　　|Asus2　　|
And though he wanted to,

　　　　　　　|Eadd9/G#
He couldn't talk to you,

|　　　　　　　　　|F#m11　　|　　　　|
He couldn't find the way.

|　　　　　　　|Bsus4　　　|　　　|　　　|
But he would always say…

Chorus 1

　　N.C.　　　‖Asus2 |E
"If I could tell her,

　　　　|C#m7　　　　|Bsus4
Tell her ev'rything I see.

　　　　|Asus2　|E
If I could tell her

　　　　　　|C#m7　　　|Bsus4
How she's ev' - rything to me.

　　|Asus2 |E　　|Bsus4　C(♭5)|C#m7　　|
But we're a million worlds a　-　part,

　|F#m11　　　　|　　　　　　|Bsus4　　|
And I don't know how I would even start.

　　　　　|E　　　|F#m11　|Asus2　　|
If I could tell her. _____

　　　　　|E　　　|F#m11　|Asus2　　|　　　　‖
If I could tell her."_____

Interlude

|E5　　　　|　　　　|A5　　　　|　　　　|
|E5　　　　|　　　　|A5　　　　|　　　‖

Verse 3

```
E5         |          |
He thought

A5            |      N.C.    |
You looked really pretty,    *err*,

A5              |
It looked pretty cool

                |E5          |          |A5          |
When you put indigo streaks in your hair.

  |E5      |      |A5                |
And he won - dered how you learned to dance

              |E5        |  |A5      |
Like all the rest of the world isn't there.
```

Pre-Chorus 2

```
              ‖C♯m7    |F♯7add4
But he kept      it all

       |Bsus4   Bsus4/A |Eadd9/G♯
In - side        his head.

            |C♯m7    |F♯7add4 |Bsus4        |
What he saw,   he left        un - said.
```

Chorus 2

```
   N.C.       ‖Asus2 |E
"If I could tell her,

          |C♯m7            |Bsus4
Tell her ev'rything I see.

          |Asus2  |E
If I could tell her

             |C♯m7         |Bsus4
How she's ev' - rything to me.

    |Asus2 |E       |Bsus4  C(♭5)|C♯m7        |
But we're a million worlds a   -    part,

   |F♯m11                  |            |Bsus4        |
And I don't know how I would even start.

            |E        |F♯m11  |Asus2      |
If I could tell her. _____
```

Bridge

```
              ‖ C        |
If I could tell her."
                        | G
But whad-da-ya do
              | D        | C        |
When there's this great divide?
              | D        |      | C        |
He just seemed so far a - way.
                        | G
And whad-da-ya do
                    | Em        | D        |
When the dis - tance is too wide?
              |          |
And how do you say,
    | Cadd9  |          |          |
"I love      you, _____
    |   |          |            |
I love you, _____
    |   |          |            |
I love you, _____
    |   |          |
I love you?" _____
```

Outro

```
              ‖ Cadd9 | G/B        | B7            | Em        |
But we're a     million   worlds a - part,
      | Am7         |                      | Dadd4⁄4          |
And I don't know how I would even start.
              | G5      | A7sus4      | Csus2        |
If I could tell her, _____
      | G5      | A7sus4          | Csus2        ‖
If I ___ could... _____
```

Disappear

Music and Lyrics by
Benj Pasek and Justin Paul

*Tune down 1/2 step:
(low to high) E♭-A♭-D♭-G♭-B♭-E♭

F♯7sus4   Asus2   Esus2   G6   Dadd2/F♯   E/G♯   Fmaj7sus♯4   C♯m

Bsus4   C   Am   G   B♭   F/A   G/B   A♭

Em   Dsus2   E♭maj7   Cm   Csus2   Dsus4   Em7   D

Intro

F♯7sus4 |**Asus2**
Guys like you and me, we're just the "losers"

                        |**Esus2** |
Who keep waiting to be seen. *Right? I mean…*

F♯7sus4 |**Asus2**
No one seems to care or stop to notice

                        |**Esus2** |
That we're there so we get lost in the inbetween.

      |**G6** |**Dadd2/F♯** |**Asus2**
But   if you can somehow keep them thinking of me

                              |**E/G♯**   **G6**|
And make me more than an a - bandoned memory,

            |**Dadd2/F♯** |
Well, that means we matter too.

            |**Fmaj7sus♯4** | ‖
It means someone will see that you are there.

* Optional to match recording.

Chorus 1

C#m |Asus2 |Bsus4 |C#m

No one deserves to be forgot - ten.

            |Asus2 |Bsus4

No one deserves to fade away.

           |F#7sus4 |Asus2

No one should come and go and have no one know

        |Esus2 |Bsus4 |C#m

He was ever even here.

           |Asus2 |Bsus4

No one deserves to disappear,

        |C   Am |

To disappear, _____

        |Esus2 | ||

Disappear.

Verse 1

Am

Even if you've always been

  |C |G

That barely-in-the-background kind of guy

  |

You still matter.

  |Am |C

And even if you're somebody who can't escape the feeling

   |G6 |

That the world's passed you by, you still matter.

  |Bb |F/A |C

If you never get around to doing some re - markable thing,

                     |G/B   Bb |

That doesn't mean that you're not worth remember - ing.

              F/A |

Think of the people who need to know.

   Ab | | ||

They need to know, so you need to show them…

Chorus 2

Em |C |Dsus2
That no one deserves to be forgot - ten.

                | |Em
No one deserves to be forgot - ten.

               |C |Dsus2
No one deserves to fade away,

               |
To fade away.

          |Am |C
No one should flicker out or have any doubt

         |G |Dsus2
That it mat - ters that they are here.

        |Em |C |Dsus2 |
No one deserves, no one deserves to disappear,

      |E♭maj7 |Cm
To disappear,

N.C. |G
Disappear.

Verse 2

         || G/B   Csus2
When you're falling in a forest

        |Dsus4 Em |G/B
And there's nobody around,

  Csus2 |Dsus4
All you want is for some - body to find you.

   |G/B   Csus2
You're falling in a forest

  |Dsus4   Em |G/B
And when you hit the ground,

      |Csus2 Dsus4 | ||
All you need is for some - body to find you.

Interlude 1

(Capo 1st fret)

|G/B Csus2 Dsus4 | Em7 |G/B Csus2 Dsus4 | |
|G/B Csus2 |Dsus4 | ||

Chorus 3

Em |Csus2 |Dsus4 |Em
  'Cause no one deserves to be forgot - ten.

          |Csus2 |Dsus4 |D ||
No one deserves to fade away.

Interlude 2

```
|Am      |C         |G              |           |
|Am      |Em   D    |G/B  Csus2  Dsus4|         |          ||
```

Chorus 4

```
Em                |C              |D              |Em
    No one deserves to be forgot - ten.
                  |C         |D              |
No one deserves to disappear
                  |Am              |C
No one should flicker out or have any doubt
                  |G              |D              |Em
That it mat - ters that they are here.
                  |C         |Dsus4      D |
No one deserves to disappear,
                  |E♭maj7        |Cm
To disappear,
          |G              |
Disappear,
                  |E♭maj7   Cm|
To disappear,
N.C.         ||
Disappear.
```

Interlude 3

```
|E♭maj7       |Cm        |G              |           |
|E♭maj7       |Cm        |G              |
```

Outro

```
                  ||E♭maj7   |Cm
To disappear,
          |G              |
Disappear.
                  |E♭maj7   |Cm
To disappear,
          |G              |
Disappear.
                  |E♭maj7   |Cm
To disappear,
          |G              |
Disappear.
                  |E♭maj7   Cm |         |N.C.
To disappear,
          ||
Disappear.
```

You Will Be Found

Music and Lyrics by
Benj Pasek and Justin Paul

*Tune down 1step:
(low to high) D-G-C-F-A-D

(Capo 1st fret)

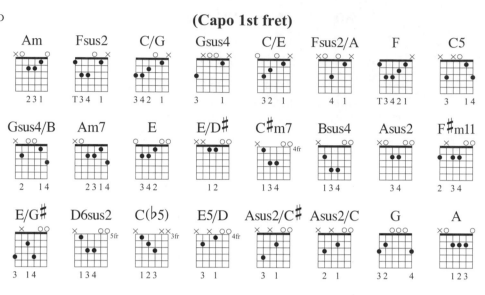

Intro |Am   Fsus2 C/G | |Am   Fsus2 C/G |

Verse 1

     ‖**Am**   **Fsus2**
Have you ever felt like

     C/G |
Nobody was there?

     |**Am**   **Fsus2**
Have you ever felt for - gotten

    |**C/G** **Gsus4**
In the middle of no - where?

     |**Am**   **Fsus2**
Have you ever felt like

     C/G |
You could disap - pear?

      |**Am**
Like you could fall

    Fsus2 |**C/G**   ‖
And no one would hear?

Interlude 1 |Am   Fsus2   C/G |

* Optional to match recording.

Verse 2

```
  ‖Am          Fsus2    C/G |            |
Well,   let that lone - ly feeling wash away.
  Am          Fsus2    C/G |          Gsus4
Maybe there's a reason to believe you'll be okay.
     |Am          Fsus2        |C/G
'Cause when you don't feel strong enough to stand,
     |Am      Fsus2 |C/G
You can reach, reach out your hand.
```

Pre-Chorus 1

```
     ‖Gsus4   C/E  Fsus2   |
And, oh,

                           Fsus2/A
Someone will come runnin',
   |Gsus4   C/E
And I know
                |F              ‖
They'll take you home.
```

Chorus 1

```
  C5                                    |Gsus4/B
    Even when the dark comes crashin' through,
                              |Am7
When you need a friend to carry you,
                              |F
And when you're broken on the ground,
         |C5
You will be found.
                         |Gsus4/B
So let the sun comes streamin' in,
                          |Am7
'Cause you'll reach up and you'll rise a - gain.
                      |F
Lift your head and look around,
         |C5            |Gsus4/B
You will be found.
         |Am7           |F
You will be found.
         |C5            |Gsus4/B
You will be found.
         |Am7           |Fsus2
You will be found.
                  ‖
You will be found.
```

Interlude 2 |C5 |Gsus4/B |Am7 |Fsus2 |

(Remove Capo)
|E |E/D♯ |C♯m7 |Asus2 |

Verse 3

Bsus4 ‖C♯m7 Asus2 |E Bsus4 |
There's a place where we don't have to feel un - known.
C♯m7 Asus2
And ev'ry time that you call out,
        |E Bsus4 |C♯m7
You're a little less alone.
        Asus2 |E Bsus4
If you on - ly say the word,
        |C♯m7 Asus2 |E ‖
From across the silence your voice is heard.

Pre-Chorus 2

Bsus4 |Asus2 |
Oh,
Bsus4 |Asus2 |
Oh,
Bsus4 |
Oh,
Asus2 |
Someone will come runnin'.
Bsus4 |Asus2 |F♯m11
Oh, _____
        | |
Oh, someone will come runnin'.
        | |Asus2
Oh, someone will come runnin'
        |
To take you home, to take you home.
        |
Someone will come runnin' to take you home,
        | ‖
To take you home, to take you home.

Chorus 2

    E |Bsus4

Even when the dark comes crashin' through,

                            |C#m7

When you need a friend to carry you,

                       |Asus2

When you're broken on the ground,

         |E

You will be found.

                       |Bsus4

So let the sun comes streamin' in,

                          |C#m7

'Cause you'll reach up and you'll rise again.

            |Asus2

If you only look around,

        |E

You will be found.

        |E/D#

You will be found.

        |E/G#

You will be found.

                 |Asus2   ‖

You will be found. You will be found.

Bridge

D6sus2 |Asus2

Out of the shadows the morning is breaking

     |E |Bsus4   C#m7

And all is new, all is new.

   |D6sus2 |Asus2

It's fillin' up the empty and suddenly I see

   |E |Bsus4   ‖

That all is new, all is new.

Breakdown

N.C. |Asus2 |

You are not alone. You are not alone.

E |Bsus4   C#m7 |

You are not alone. You are not alone.

F#m11 |Asus2 |

You are not alone. You are not alone.

E   Bsus4 |

You are not, you are not a - lone.

            ‖

You are not alone.

Chorus 3

    E |E/D♯
        Even when the dark comes crashin' through,

                                         |C♯m7
When you need someone to carry you,

                          Asus2 |
When you're broken on the ground,

N.C. |E
You will be found.

                              |Bsus4
So let the sun comes streamin' in,

                         C(♭5) |C♯m7
'Cause you'll reach up and you'll rise again.

                    |Asus2
If you only look around,

              |E
You will be found.

                              |Bsus4
Even when the dark comes crashin' through,

        |C♯m7
You will be found.

                            |Asus2
When you need someone to carry you,

        |E5/D |Aadd2/C♯
You will be found.

        |Asus2/C |N.C.
You will be found.

            ‖
You will be found.

Outro |C♯m7 Asus2 E | |G |
                   |A |E | ‖

To Break in a Glove

Music and Lyrics by
Benj Pasek and Justin Paul

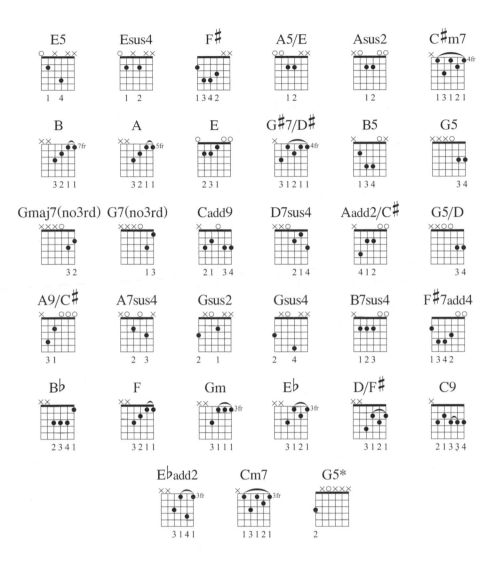

Intro

E5   Esus4   N.C.
                 (This glove is really cool, wow.)

(Why don't you take it?)

 E5   Esus4   N.C.
(Oh, no, no, I couldn't.)

(Why not?) (Are you sure?)

Verse 1

```
       E5           Esus4  N.C.
         I bought this glove
         |F♯         N.C.
A thousand years ago
       |A5/E              N.C.
For some birthday or some Christmas
       |E5               Esus4  N.C.|E5
That has come and gone.
         Esus4          N.C.         |
I thought we might play catch or…
F♯            N.C.
I don't know,
       |A5/E             N.C.
But he left it in the bag
         |E5       Esus4
With the tag still on.
  N.C.                    |
(You'll have to break it in, though, first.
                              |E5       Esus4
You can't catch anything with it that stiff.)
  N.C.          |                 ||
(How do you break it in?) Well,
```

Verse 2

```
E5        Esus4          |F♯
   It's all a process that is really quite precise,
       |A5/E                         |E5  Esus4
A sort of secret method known to very few.
     |E5              Esus4  |F♯
So,    if you're in the market for professional advice,
       |A5/E        Asus2           ||
Well, to - day could be a lucky day for you.
```

Interlude 1

          E5   **Esus4**   **N.C.** |
                          (Shaving cream.) (Shaving cream?)

                                          |**E5**
(Oh yeah. You rub that in for about five minutes.

Esus4   **N.C.** |
Tie it all up with rubber bands,

                                          |
Put in under your mattress and sleep on it.

E5   **Esus4**   **N.C.** |
And you do that for at least a week, every day. Consistent.)

Pre-Chorus

               ||**C♯m7**   **B**
And though this method isn't easy,
   |**A**   **E**   **G♯7/D♯**|**C♯m7**
Ev'ry second that you spend is gonna pay off.
   F♯ |**B5**
It'll pay off in the end.

Chorus 1

      ||**G5** |**Gmaj7(no3rd)**
It just takes a little patience.
                |**G7(no3rd)**
It takes a little time,
                  |**Cadd9**
A little perseverance and a little uphill climb.
   |**G5**
You might not think it's worth it,
   |**D7sus4**
You might begin to doubt,
   |**Cadd9** |**Aadd2/C♯**
But you can't take any shortcuts,

You gotta stick it out.
      |**G5/D**
And it's the hard way,
    |**A9/C♯**
But it's the right way,
  |**A7sus4 D7sus4**|
The right   way
         ||
To break in a glove.

                                 Gsus2   Gsus4   N.C.
Interlude 2   *(With something like this,*
                                         |
                                 You have to be ready to put in the work.
                                                      |Gsus2 Gsus4 N.C.
                                 Make the commitment.)
                                         |
                                 (So, what do you think?)
                                                B7sus4 ‖
                                 (I mean, definitely.)

                                 E |F♯7add4
Verse 3   Some people say, "Just use a microwave.
                                       |Asus2 |E
                                 Or try that 'Run-it-through-hot-water' technique."
                                       | |F♯7add4
                                 Well, they can gloat about the time they save
                                       |Asus2 |E
                                 'Til they gotta buy another glove next week.

                                     ‖G5
Chorus 2   It just takes a little patience,
                                   |Gmaj7(no3rd) |G7(no3rd)
                                 It takes a little time,
                                                      |Cadd9
                                 A little perseverance and a little uphill climb.
                                       |G5/D |A9/C♯
                                 And it's the hard way but it's the right way,
                                     |Cadd9 D7sus4 |
                                 The right   way.

Bridge

|| **B♭** | **F** | **Gm**
'Cause there's a right way in ev'rything you do.

| **E♭**
Keep that grit,

|
Follow through.

| **F**   **Gm**   **F** | **E♭**
Even when ev - 'ryone around you thinks you're crazy,

| **F**   **Gm**   **F** | **E♭**
Even when ev - 'ryone around you lets things go.

| **F**   **Gm**
Whether you're prepping for some test,

| **E♭**
Or you're miles from some goal,

| **F**   **D/F♯**
Or you're just trying to do what's best

| **Gm**   **B♭** | **E♭**
For a kid who's lost con - trol.

| **B♭** | **C9**
You do the hard thing 'cause that's the right thing,

| **E♭add2** **Cm7** | ||
Yeah, that's the right   thing.

Interlude 3

Gsus2 **Gsus4** **N.C.** |
        (Connor was really lucky

|
To have a dad that...
  Gsus2 **Gsus4** **N.C.** |
A dad who cared so much about

| **Gsus2**   **Gsus4** **N.C.**
Taking care of stuff.)

(Shaving cream. Rubber bands.

|
Mattress. Repeat. Got it?)

(Got it.)

Outro

|| **G5/D** | **A9/C♯**
It's the hard way, but it's the right way,

| **A7sus4** **D7sus4** |
The right   way

| **Gsus2**   **Gsus4** |
To break in a glove.

| **G5*** **N.C.** ||
(You're good to go.)

Only Us

Music and Lyrics by
Benj Pasek and Justin Paul

(Capo 2nd fret)

Asus2 E5 Emaj7 C#m7 F#m11 B7add4 G#7/B# F#7add4 Bsus4

G5 D5 B5 Bmaj7(no3rd) G#m7 F#11/A# D#7/G C#7 C#sus2

A#m7 D#m F# C# A G#7sus4 G#7 G# F#add9

Intro
|Asus2 | |E5 | |
|Asus2 | |E5 | ||

Verse 1

Asus2 |
   I don't need you to sell me
       |E5 | |Asus2
On reasons to want you.
       |
I don't need you to search
       |E5 |Emaj7 E5 |C#m7
For the proof that I   should.
       |F#m11 |B7add4
You don't have to con - vince me.
       |E5 G#7/B# |C#m7
You don't have to be scared you're not enough
   |F#7add4 |Bsus4 | ||
'Cause what we've got goin'   is good.

Verse 2

Asus2 |
  I don't need more reminders
      |E5 |Emaj7 E5 |Asus2
Of all that's been broken.
        |
I don't need you to fix
      |E5 |Emaj7 E5 |C♯m7 |
What I'd rather forget.
        |F♯m11 |B7add4
Clear the slate and start over.
       |E5 G♯7/B♯ |C♯m7 |
Try to clear the noises in your head.
F♯7add4 |Bsus4 | ||
We can't compete with all that.

Chorus 1

E5 |
  So what if it's us?
     |C♯m7| |F♯m11
What if it's us and only us?
       |
And what came before
       |B7add4 |
Won't count anymore, or matter.
       |E5
Can we try that?
      |
What if it's you?
     |C♯m7
What if it's me?
      | |G5
And what if that's all that we need it to be,
     | D5 |F♯m11 |B7add4
And the rest of the world falls a - way?
       ||
What do you say?

Verse 3

E5 |
I never thought there'd be someone like you
   |B5 |Bmaj7(no3rd) B5
Who would want me.
   |E5
So I give you ten thousand reasons
      |B5 |Bmaj7(no3rd) B5 |G♯m7
To not let me go.
       |C♯m7 |F♯11/A♯
But if you really see me,
        |B5 D♯7/G |G♯m7
If you like me for me and nothing else,
      |C♯7
Well, that's all that I've wanted
  |F♯7add4 | ‖
For longer than you could possibly know.

Chorus 2

B5 |
  So it can be us.
    |G♯m7 | |C♯m7
It can be us and only us.
        |
And what came before
       |F♯7add4 |
Won't count anymore or matter.
     |E5
We can try that.
    | |G♯m7
It's not so impossi - ble.
  |F♯7add4 |E5
Nobody else but the two of us here.
        | |G♯m7
'Cause you're saying it's possi - ble.
     |F♯7add4 |E5
We can just watch the whole world disappear
  | |G♯m7 |F♯7add4 |
'Til you're the only one I
C♯m7 | |F♯7add4 |
Still know how to see.
       ‖
It's just you and me.

Chorus 3

C#sus2 |
It'll be us.
   |A#m7 | |D#m
It'll be us and only us.

        |
And what came before
        |F# |
Won't count anymore.
      |C# |
We can try that
   |A#m7
You and me.
   | |E5
That's all that we need it to be.
     | B5 |A
And the rest of the world falls away.
    |E5   B5 |G#7sus4 |G#7 |G#7sus4 |
And the rest of the world falls away.

Outro

     ‖C# |A#m7
The world falls away.
    |C# |A#m7
The world falls away
   |C# |A#m7 G# |F#add9 |C#   ‖
And it's only us.

Good for You

Music and Lyrics by
Benj Pasek and Justin Paul

(Capo 1st fret)

Bm7   Gsus2   Dsus2   Em7   Cadd9   Cmaj7   C#5   A/C#

Asus4   A   F#7   D/F#   A5   E5   B5   G#7

Intro |**Bm7 Gsus2** |**Dsus2** |**Bm7 Gsus2** |**Dsus2** ||

Verse 1

Bm7   **Gsus2** |**Dsus2** |**Bm7**
    So you found a place where the grass is greener,

              Gsus2 |**Dsus2**

And you jumped the fence to the other side.

    |**Em7**

Is it good?

               |**Cadd9**   **Cmaj7** |**Bm7**

Are they giving you a world I could never pro - vide?

Gsus2 |**Dsus2**   **C#5** ||

Verse 2

Bm7   **Gsus2** |**Dsus2**   **A/C#** |**Bm7**
    Well, I hope you're proud of your big decision.

            Gsus2 |**Dsus2**

Yeah, I hope it's all that you want and more.

    |**Em7**   **Bm7** |

Now you're free from the agonizing life

        Asus4   **A** |**Gsus2** ||

You were liv - ing be - fore.

Pre-Chorus 1

Em7 |Bm7
And you say what you need to say

                       |Em7
So that you get to walk away.

                   Bm7 |
It would kill you to have to stay trapped

          Asus4 A |Em7
When you've got   somethin' new.

                  |Bm7
Well, I'm sorry you had it rough,

             Cadd9 |
And I'm sorry I'm not enough.

        |F♯7 ||
Thank God they res - cued you.

Chorus 1

Gsus2   Dsus2 |Asus4
So you got what you always wanted.

        Bm7
So you got your dream-come-true.

 |Gsus2 Dsus2 |
Well, good for you.

Asus4   Bm7 Asus4
Good for you,   you.

Gsus2 | Dsus2 |Asus4
You got a taste of a life so perfect.

        Bm7 |
So you did what you had to do.

Gsus2   Dsus2 |
Good for you.

F♯7 ||
Good for you.

Interlude

|Bm7 Gsus2 |Dsus2   A/C♯ ||

Verse 3

```
Bm7                   Gsus2                |Dsus2   A/C♯ |Bm7
    Does it cross your mind to be slightly sor - ry?
              Gsus2            |Dsus2
Do you even care that you might be      wrong?
        |Em7
Was it fun?
                          Bm7 |          Asus4   A     Gsus2 |              ||
Well, I hope you had a blast  while you dragged me a - long.
```

Pre-Chorus 2

```
Em7                                    |Bm7
    And you say what you need to say
                                  |Em7
And you play who you need to play.

And if somebody's in your way,
Bm7 |          Asus4  A         |Em7
Crush them and leave    them behind.
                        |Bm7
Well, I guess if I'm not of use.
                        |Cadd9
Go ahead you can cut me loose.
        |F♯7           ||
Go ahead now, I won't mind.
```

Bridge 1

```
Gsus2                          |Dsus2
    I'll shut my mouth and I'll let    you go.
        |Asus4
Is that good for you?
              |Em7          D/F♯  Gsus2 |
Would that be good for you, you,    you?
                          |Dsus2
I'll just sit back while you run the show.
        |Asus4
Is that good for you?
              |Em7          D/F♯  Gsus2 ||
Would that be good for you, you,    you?
```

Bridge 2

Gsus2 |Dsus2
    All I need is some time to think

                      |Asus4
But the boat is about to sink.

                 |Em7
Can't erase what I wrote in ink.

              D/F$\sharp$ Gsus2 |
Tell me how I can change the story?

                |Dsus2
All the words that I can't take back,

             |Em7
Like a train comin' off the track

             |F$\sharp$7
As the rails and the bolts all crack.

             |
I gotta find a way to stop it! Stop it!

N.C.   A5 ‖
Just let me out.

Chorus 2

A5   E5 |B5
    So you got what you always wanted.

          C$\sharp$5 |
So you got your dream-come-true.

A5   E5 |
Good for you,

      C$\sharp$5 B5
Good for you, you.

A5 | E5 |B5
You got a taste of a life so perfect.

          C$\sharp$5 |
Now you say that you're someone new.

A5   E5 |
Good for you.

G$\sharp$7 |
Good for you.

A5   E5 |
Good for you.

G$\sharp$7 | A5 |N.C.
Good for you.

               |C$\sharp$5   ‖
So you got what you always wanted.

Words Fail

Music and Lyrics by
Benj Pasek and Justin Paul

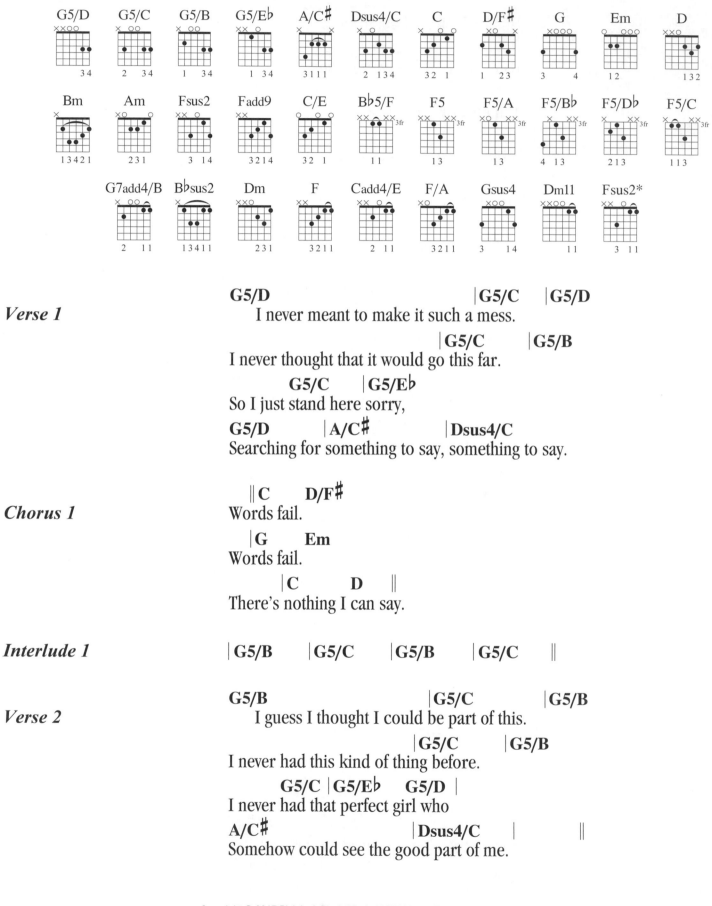

Verse 1

|G5/D |G5/C |G5/D

I never meant to make it such a mess.

                  |G5/C |G5/B

I never thought that it would go this far.

      G5/C |G5/Eb

So I just stand here sorry,

G5/D |A/C# |Dsus4/C

Searching for something to say, something to say.

Chorus 1

      ‖C   D/F#

Words fail.

    |G   Em

Words fail.

     |C   D   ‖

There's nothing I can say.

Interlude 1

|G5/B |G5/C |G5/B |G5/C   ‖

Verse 2

G5/B |G5/C |G5/B

I guess I thought I could be part of this.

              |G5/C |G5/B

I never had this kind of thing before.

      G5/C |G5/Eb G5/D |

I never had that perfect girl who

A/C# |Dsus4/C | ‖

Somehow could see the good part of me.

Verse 3

G5/B |G5/C |G5/B
I never had the dad who stuck it out:

                  |G5/C |
No corny jokes or base - ball gloves.

G5/B   G5/C |G5/Eb
No mom who just was there,

        G5/D |A/C# |D ||
'Cause "Mom" was all that she had to be.

Pre-Chorus 1

Em |C |
That's not a worthy explanation:

G |D/F# |Em
I know there is none.

                |Bm
Nothing can make sense

              |Am |
Of all these things I've done.

Chorus 2

  G5/B ||C   D/F#
Words   fail.

 |G Em
Words fail.

     |Fsus2 |Fadd9
There's nothing I can say

          G5/B |C
Except, some - times you see ev'rything you wanted.

 |Fadd9 G5/B |C
And sometimes you see ev'rything you wish you had,

  |Fadd9   G
And it's right there,

       |
Right there,

Am G |Em   Fadd9 |
Right there in front of you.

              |Em   Fadd9
And you want to be - lieve it's true,

     |Em   Fsus2 |Am
So you   make it true, and you think,

     C   Em |Fsus2 |
Maybe ev'ry - body wants it,

              |
Needs it

  C/E ||
A little bit…

Interlude 2

```
              Fadd9              |Bb5/F           |
              Too.
              |F5                |Bb5/F           |
              |F5/A     F5/Bb    |F5/Db   F5/C    |
              |G7add4/B          |              |Bbsus2        ||
```

Pre-Chorus 2

Dm |Bbsus2 |F
  This was just a sad invention.

                |Cadd4/E |Dm
It wasn't real,   I know.

                  |Am
But we were happy,

                |Bbsus2 |
I guess I couldn't let that go.

              |F/A |
I guess I couldn't give that up.

                |Dm
I guess I wanted to believe

              |Cadd4/E
'Cause if I just believe,

                 |Bbsus2 |Dm
Then I don't have to see what's really there.

                 |
No, I'd rather pretend I'm something better

      |Bbsus2
Than these broken parts.

    |F |Cadd4/E
Pre - tend I'm something other than this mess that I am,

            |Dm
'Cause then I don't have to look at it,

     |Bbsus2
And no one gets to look at it.

 |F/A |Cadd4/E ||
No, no one can real - ly see.

Bridge

Am |F   Gsus4 |C/E
     'Cause I've learned to slam on the brake

     F |Gsus4 |Am
Before I even turn the key,

     F |Gsus4 |C/E
Before I make the mistake,

     F |Am   Gsus4
Before I lead with the worst of me.

|C/E   F |Am |G
I never let them see the worst of me.

|C/E   F Gsus4 |

                      |F   Gsus4 |
'Cause what if ev'ryone saw?

             |C/E F Gsus4 |
What if everyone knew?

                    |F
Would they like what they saw,

     |F/A   Gsus4 |Dm11
Or would they hate it too? |

     |Am   Gsus4   C/E   F
Will I just keep on running a - way   from what's true?

Am |F |Gsus4
All I ever do is run,

     |Dm11   Fsus2* |
So how do I step in,

Outro

                   C   Dm11 ‖Fsus2* | |
Step into the sun? _____

|C   Dm11   Fsus2* |
           |C   Dm11   Fsus2*| ‖
Step into the sun? _____

‖: C   Dm11   Fsus2* | :‖ *Play 3 times*

So Big/So Small

Music and Lyrics by
Benj Pasek and Justin Paul

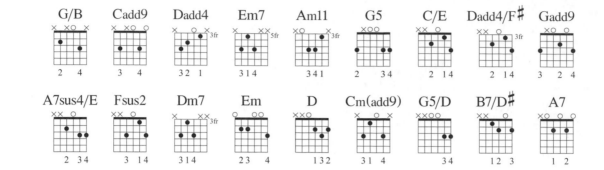

Intro

‖: G/B   Cadd9 | Dadd4   :‖

Verse 1

G/B   Cadd9 | Dadd4
   It was a February day

       | G/B   Cadd9
When your dad came by

      | Dadd4 | Em7
Before goin'   a - way.

      Dadd4 | Am11
A U-haul truck in the driveway:

    | Dadd4 | G5   ‖
The day it was suddenly real.

Verse 2

G/B   Cadd9 | Dadd4
   I told you not to come out - side

      | G/B   Cadd9
But you saw that truck

    | Dadd4
And you smiled so wide.

  | Em7   Dadd4 | Am11 | Dadd4
A real live truck in your driveway:

           | G5
We let you sit behind the wheel.

Pre-Chorus

      ‖**C/E** **Dadd4/F♯** |
Good - bye

Gadd9
Goodbye.

 |**Cadd9** **G/B** |
Now it's just me

 A7sus4/E **Fsus2**
And my little guy.

Chorus 1

     ‖**Dm7 Cadd9** |**Gadd9**
And the house felt so big.

    |**Dm7 Cadd9** |**Gadd9**
And I felt so small.

    |**Dm7 Cadd9** |**Gadd9**
The house felt so big

    |**Dm7 Cadd9** |**G5**   ‖
And I felt so small.

Verse 3

G/B   **Cadd9** |**Dadd4**
  That night I tucked you into bed,

 |**G/B**   **Cadd9**
I will never for - get

    |**Dadd4**
How you sat up and said,

      |**Em7**   **Dadd4** |**Am11**
"Is there an - other truck comin' to our driveway,

 |**Dadd4** |**G5**
A truck that will take Mommy a - way?"

Chorus 2

     ‖**Dm7 Cadd9** |**Gadd9**
And the house felt so big

   |**Dm7 Cadd9** |**Gadd9**
And I felt so small.

   |**Dm7 Cadd9** |**Gadd9**
The house felt so big.

   |**Dm7**
And I . . .

Bridge

   ‖ **Cadd9** |**Em**   **D**
And I knew there would be moments that I'd miss.

    |**Cadd9** |**Em**   **D**
And I knew there would be space I couldn't fill.

    |**Cadd9** |**Cm(add9)**   **G/B**
And I knew I'd come up short a million diff'rent ways.

    |**G5/D**
And I did,

    |**C/E**
And I do,

    |**Dadd4/F♯**   ‖
And I will.

Verse 4

    G/B   **Cadd9** |**Dadd4**
   But like that February day,

    |**G/B**   **Cadd9**
I will take your hand,

     |**Dadd4**
Squeeze it tightly and say,

      |**Em7**   **Dadd4** |**Am11**
 "There's not another truck in the drive - way.

    |**G/B**
Your mom isn't goin' anywhere.

    |**Cadd9**
Your mom is stayin' right here."

    |**Dadd4**
Your mom isn't goin' anywhere.

    |**B7/D♯**
Your mom is stayin' right here.

     |**Em** |**G/B**
No matter what I'll be here

Chorus 3

      ‖ **Dm7** **Cadd9** |**Gadd9**
When it all   feels so big

    |**Dm7** **Cadd9** |**Gadd9**
'Til it all   feels so ____ small.

    |**Dm7** **Cadd9** |**Gadd9**
When it all   feels so big

    |**Dm7 Cadd9** |**Em**   **A7**
'Til it all feels   so ____ small.

    |**Dadd4**   ‖
'Til it all feels so…

Outro

    G/B   **Cadd9** |**Dadd4** |
Small. _____

|**G/B**   **Cadd9** |**Dadd4** |**G5**   ‖